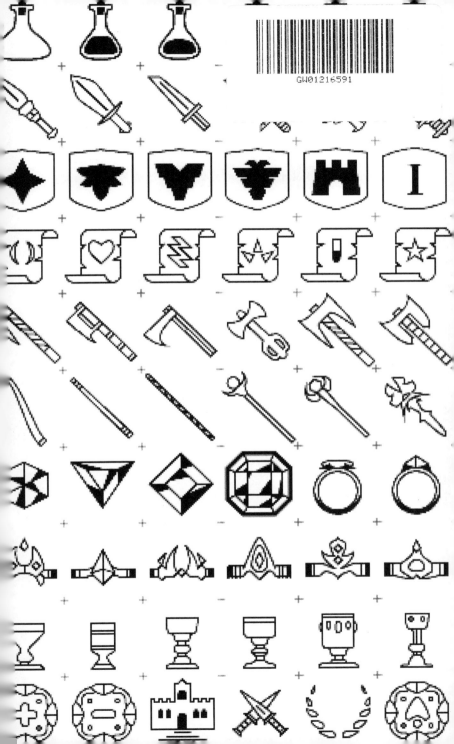

Also by Liam Bates

Monomaniac (Broken Sleep Books, 2021)

Working Animals (Broken Sleep Books, 2020)

HUMAN TOWNSPERSON

Bates

© 2022 Liam Bates. All rights reserved; no part of this book may be reproduced by any means without the publisher's permission.

ISBN: 978-1-915079-24-4

The author has asserted their right to be identified as the author of this Work in accordance with the Copyright, Designs and Patents Act 1988

Cover designed by Aaron Kent

Edited and typeset by Aaron Kent

Broken Sleep Books Ltd
Rhydwen,
Talgarreg,
SA44 4HB
Wales

Contents

Character Building	11
What I Did Over the Summer	12
Enchantments & Curiosities	13
Night-time Visitor	14
Delicately Balanced	16
Plume	17
Broadside	18
Giver	19
A Decade of Grazing	21
The Taster	22
Bargaining	24
On Their Radar	25
Blackbirds	26
Fetch Quest	27
Self-Care	28
At the school for assassins	29
After the Attack	32
The Protagonist	35
Washed Up by the River	36
How I Keep Getting Myself	37

Posture and Grip	38
The Midwife	39
Spoils	40
Apprentice/Master	41
Oral History	43
Hero Training	45
Hearth	46
A Path	47
The Agency	51
Understudy	52
Compulsions	53
Aubade with Forecast	54
His Echocardiogram Looks Good Now	55
Missing Years	56
Open Wide, a Little Wider	57
Something Came Up, Be There Soon	58
Acknowledgements	61

Human Townsperson

Liam Bates

For Katie

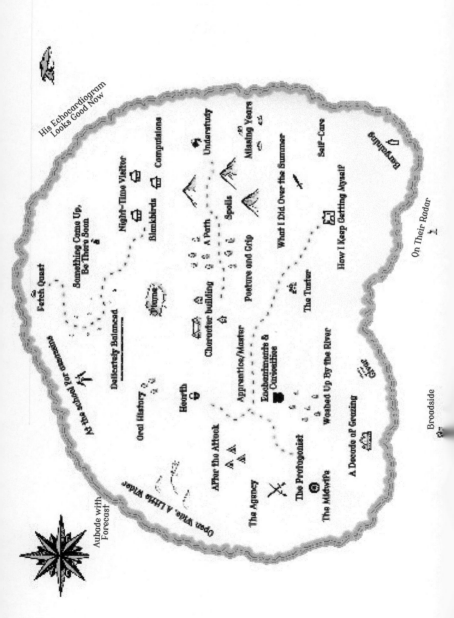

I

They entered no mysterious domain. Nothing happened.
— *The Wizard of Earthsea*, Ursula K. Le Guin

Character Building

You were mumbling something angsty. Was it
that same dream, the one with options?

I know you hate waking, but this letter came
first thing. See the wax seal?

I guess you went to sleep in your clothes
again, forgot to flip the light off. Does that mean

you're ready? If the answer's yes, blink twice
like there's an ice chip lodged in your eyelid

you're endeavouring to melt.
If the answer's yes, turn to the window

and cough. Are you coughing
to show readiness, or is it

the smoke? The blacksmith, assuming their workshop
survives, can supply you with a weapon

to defend yourself. For now, take this
life-sized anatomical model

of the human brain. If you made good choices
before this point, you'll know what to do.

What I Did Over the Summer

Imagine fly-tipping a medieval longsword
or at least an artisanal replica in a
skip at the roadside like some busted umbrella.
I've got metal polish in a drawer. I could
lug it home, make it into furniture.
Do you remember how we used to
make furniture of everything? But
before any concrete decision,
it starts to snow, all around me, thin flakes
of white. Orange, wait, it's not snow. A
cannabis factory on the corner
must have shorted and
caught fire. Warm ash on my tongue.
What furniture would I even make—
a hat stand? Imagine the reaction
if I started wearing hats again.
It's not like my parents don't already
have enough to worry about.

Enchantments & Curiosities

This one wants a dagger and shield.
The next wants dynamite, granola bars
or rope. Health potions are a must.
I keep the shelves tidy and floor swept.
Whenever the bell above the door
trills: *how might I be of service?*

Proto-heroes leave grinning
like takeaway drunks with deeply fried orders.
My diet's simple. In bed by ten.

Once a year, I yield to a holiday, leafy green,
near the water. Sitting on the lakeshore for my wife
to snap me with ice cream cone, rainbow sprinkles.
Apparently, I'm rigid—in an odd sense, not
like a monument. It wouldn't do to get comfy.

Of the last batch of customers, victors
will drop back to boast livid scars, fractured
bones and stolen relics, flush for repeat sales.
Many won't, annihilated in last stands

or a miscellaneous gory fate, I wonder
if it's true what I've read, how at the end
there's a warmth like waking to sunshine,
sheathed in blankets, forgetting where you are.

Night-time Visitor

'We hypothesized that highly emotional mouse strains, such as the BALB/c and DBA/2, might exhibit sensitivity to chronic fluoxetine treatment.'
— Dulawa, Holick, Gunderson and Hen (2004)

What I first took
to be a fruit
gone furry at the bottom of the bin,

didn't feel right. An odour,
vaguely piscine. Peering closer

at the limp grey matter in my hands
I spotted the four feet, the long tail.
A field mouse,
according to the internet. Crawled inside
to search for water, a neighbour

must've sown poison. Couldn't swallow
my sobs. First wet cry
for ages. Medication
side effects normally
deny the release. While waiting

for 3-to-5-working-day delivery
mesh to barricade the hole,
I managed
to discover a second mouse
scrabbling in our non-lethal trap
—released him into undergrowth
well away from everyone.

Now the entry's covered—
the circumference of the end
of a pencil is all that's needed
for the natural order to creep in.
The noises I twitch at,
squeaks and scratches,
have mundane explanations:
a loved one sliding
a chair across the floorboards.
A kid next door who needs to run

in circles. But can't shake this
lingering awareness of my self,
how a mouse might understand us,
enormous clattering
shadow over everything.

Delicately Balanced

The whole borough's gathered in the square
for the latest execution.

Those who were extra keen cling
to their places at the front.

A song like a hymn spreads concentric
from a segment of the crowd.

When the sun slips free from a last lump
of white cloud, this

skyward cheer combines with the spritz
of summer fruit cider and SPF 30. Still,

a few fringe spectators are critical:
What a sorry state, they say, *such a state*

that public entertainment's in. Pleased
it isn't them though, with their neck bared

on the block. I'm grateful quite simply
to be noticed in a breathing

mass. I can't see his eyes, but for definite
the executioner is focused on me.

He's resting his axe at an angle like
a minute hand nearing five

and it's almost time for me
to gather my things and head off.

Plume

In the alleyway we go to smoke,
it happens again. I don't know why
it's so often fire that does for me; this grey
burning taste lingers, in spite of teeth cleans
and meals eaten. Did I do either yet today?
It doesn't matter. Nothing so glamorous
as a dragon or wizard. It's your basic
spontaneous combustion. Another flash added
to the night's motley, then the spark's gone.
Companions stand above me like stoned angels,
guarding my remains from scavengers, waiting
for revival. There's a thing with feathers
they do ordinarily: downy feathers from the tail
of an endangered bird. But with recent strains
on resurrection services—they're fresh out.
Instead, a wait. It might be hours
until I pull myself together, against entropy
and updrafts, from disparate matter
that could by now be miles apart.
And their watch never wavers,
though I must make lonely company.

Broadside

Of all days, the crew choose today
to stage a mutiny.
Their cutlasses bright
curves like smiles of laboured courtesy.
No need for awkward discussion. Of course
I volunteer to plank-walk into the drink.
I'll tread water until
my legs betray me or a hammerhead
favours me with a pity kill.
See, this is exactly what the problem is,
they say, *that's obviously not what we want.*
Gawping as if at an albatross
with a six-pack's plastic rings round his neck.
Haven't I risked my life to keep us
awash with grog and treasure?
Sure you have, they say,
but what have you risked that matters to you?

Giver

You look like someone
who can handle themselves.
Do you think you could help

to rid me of this bearded man
who looms in my bedroom window
when I'm trying to get the hang of how
to change my base metal into treasure?

You look like someone
with a good sense of where they're going.
Do you think you could help

retrieve a gold pendant I misplaced?
It contains the last of my prescription.
I had it with me in a strobelit warehouse
on the dim and swirling side of the city.
I guess it slipped off my sweaty neck.
Not sure how I found myself there
or how to get back.

You look like someone
familiar. Did I do it again,
did I forget your face? Did I gorge myself
and forget what to call you?

You look like someone
who knows their way round a kitchen.
Do you feel like dinner? I'm limited
to making meals from leaves and mud.

Could you hold my head
in your hands like a river
holds a twig when it drops from the bridge?

A Decade of Grazing

My tutor said I showed real promise
walking on all fours
and snipping clumps of grass,
teeth acquainted with grinding, but
I only joined a few classes
before e-mailing sincere
apologies. The excuses

got lazy: the dog ate my alarm clock,
a warlock put a curse on me,
it's honestly my shadow
who you're after.
Until I stopped bothering entirely.

Periodically, I'll find an ex-classmate online
and nose through their feed.
A lot of them are doing well,
especially George,
who is a piebald horse now.
Click-clacking through pictures.

Him in a field.
Him walking down a dirt track,
trees in pink blossom either side.
Him in a stable.

The Taster

A buffet spread
of HD recordings:

he dives
on a foot-long sub with tainted mayo
like a hero embracing a grenade,
spotting flecks of red against the porcelain.

When others would quit,
he swallows ten sachets of salt
stirred in water from the tap behind the bar,
voids his contents. More
room free to sample
every liquid in a two-mile radius. Exhausted
in the road and spirited away
by nearby blue siren-lights.

Letters on the mat.
He shreds and swallows them,
shits confetti for a week.

He checks dubious gin
just in case, sits blackout
in the afternoon, streaming
in the curtain-cut light: a docuseries
of iffy credibility.

His face the picture of clarity—
assassins could be hidden
in the mask of any napping friend,

finds a secret bag of powder,
necks it like sherbet,
converts the mixture to a dark stain
across the mattress. A toxin successfully
neutralised.

Lips blue
like paintings of a deity,
ready to go forth, he asks
the paramedics hanging over him
if he might get a lift to the hospital.

Two of him face-to-face with
throats extended gulping
a clutch of pharmaceuticals, two
grimaces, one inverted
by the mirrored bathroom cabinet.

Except, an intruder must have
tampered with the footage.
Lacking context, his actions
make not a spot of sense.
There's no sign of the people
he remembers protecting.

Bargaining

A man with a corner stall
at the Monday bric-a-brac market
is offering the power of flight
in exchange for a fondest memory.

Lunch break on the metal bench opposite,
I admire buyers
adjusting to their new wings,
thin flaps of skin like a bat's,
before they kick off from the cobblestones.

Most attempt a flourish like a loop-the-loop,
allowing themselves a snatch
of upsidedownness before vanishing
behind the spire of the cathedral.

I savour my sandwich and imagine it:
the world opening underneath me.

My normal train cancelled,
I'll simply stretch my wings and take
to the sky without thinking. I'll speed
across the city on thermals

and come down nice and easy
into the car park, as Nick's
arriving in his silver Honda Civic
and he'll say, *Wow, you're here early*
and I'll say, *Yeah, I guess it is pretty early.*

On Their Radar

When heavy wind is forecast, I slink outside
when the neighbourhood is sleeping.
Nobody sees me tipping bins and throwing
litter into hedges. Nobody sees me
pruning phone lines with secateurs,
although come morning they'll notice
the light on their router's gone orange
and maybe their day's improved. Me
vaulting their side gate,
kicking down a fence panel,
capsizing the trampoline, the table
reimagined as koi pond white plastic ornament.
It's not the recognition, it's the effort
that's important, hence the town meeting
when the mayor infers we have strayed
and incurred the disapproval of the gods,
a sacrifice may be in order,
would anyone volunteer themselves
to begin making amends
for our transgressions, I nod along
but I do not step forward.

Blackbirds

The ones we have
brooding in the eaves
lost two more chicks. I found them,
abject and pink on the patio.
There must be a moment
where a hatchling clearly won't make it
past this scrotal stage—their bodies
jettisoned from the nest. Of every ten eggs,
only four will strike out on their own. I couldn't
let the cat find them, so shrouded
both inside a tissue for
the outside bin. Recently,
when I got too sick and
chucked it all in again, Dad appeared
at my flat. He collected the dishes
and dirty clothes I'd left nestled
and did a load of washing while I slept.
He even scrubbed the bathroom, and pulled
a wad of pubes and soap and feathers
from the plughole. If I'm too far gone,
he wipes it clean. He has this bulky chest
in my old bedroom for storing
important records: certificates, licences,
a recent bill or two. A crude false
bottom hides a book of matches;
with every major reset, a head ignites and
one match burns down to black wood.
How many in reserve? He's never told me
and I've never asked.

Fetch Quest

In town, a hooded figure with a white-collared cloak gave exact directions where to find my missing children, though they've not been born yet. Hidden not far from here, sealed in a shadowy cave. I think it might be best if I let them be for now. Bringing them into this light, having to field their questions, the curious black dots of their eyes, where even to begin.

Self-Care

On your advice, I drew myself
a steaming bath with scented oils
and lay down in the water
like lentils soaking overnight.

The ache began to ease.
I felt my torso untighten.

Under bubbles though for so long,
when I resurfaced and wrapped
in a towel, it was clear I'd washed
the opacity from my skin.
It spiralled away with the water.

Now I cast a cellophane-pink shadow.
In a well-lit room or bright weather
the curl of my internal organs
becomes apparent, pulsating
for anyone to see.

I've started sleeping in a woolly hat,
pulling it down past my eyebrows.
I don't want you to know
the banality of my dreams.

At the school for assassins

                    they had us
studying piano drop montages
for hours at a time: every gram
of their bodies aching to return
to ground level, the pulley
snap, the flattened passersby
or phew-that-was-closes.
An upright emits a wooden
gasp, then bassy resonance
dampens to hum to
meet the tone of our breaths.
Better students moved on
to sharper concerns, the finer points
of dagger upkeep, the eight
fatal strike points. We stayed
in the projection room past nightfall,
permanent imprints
in the beanbags, falling
behind. We left
with no diploma, but can judge
if a baby grand wants tuning by the timbre
as it smashes into asphalt.

At a party full of old classmates,
now contract killers of note, us dropouts
insisted on an icebreaker game
of wink murder. Your body
percussion on the floor,
a painterly pose, with Buckfast
pooling where you let it fall.

I hijacked the playlist, swapping
Tom Petty for industrial techno
and after that is blackness.

The last time we talked,
I'd let the few miles
between us elongate. We hid
from tipsy acquaintances on the balcony.
The moon appeared as a bright pebble
dropped into a well, to check for the splash
that proves nothing's bottomless.
Before I left, to pedal back
along a clear canal path
you held me long and hard.
When Alex called, weeks later,

the room went monochrome. Sounds
muffled, as if through felt.
My voice dropped
to a creaking register.
I never learnt
which bridge exactly.
Whenever I cycle
beneath one, there's this jolt
and I get off to push, a
stiff half-step then its echo,
till my blood stops buzzing.

When a human falls like that,
a piece breaks off the world,
like with each heavy rain
this rented house gets
thinner.
You never expected

me present at the railing
or as crumple zone below
to cushion the thud.
I apologise often regardless

to your digital shadow,
for falling back. My messages
remain unread, stack higher
like scaffolding braced against the wind:
A video of a cat you would've liked,
that stupid song was playing in the taxi,
I found a baggy two-thirds white
on the floor of the cubicle
and pictured you behind the stall divider
saying, *Don't think about it.*
And it's good to hear
your voice and feel that familiar
weight in my hand

After the Attack

The campsite was still standing.
You produced that battered set
of travel chess, as if nothing had happened.
As if all in the vicinity hadn't listened
to final confessions of my every fuck up.
A speck of air-light ash settled in my trouser cuff
but it was only Roz frying vegetarian sausages.
She was singing some upbeat pop hook.
It didn't make sense, my persisting.
The forest shook,
didn't it? The psychopomps collared me,
didn't they? Skidding into sight
in flashing vans. Yet, here was the sun's refutation
on the valley, grass become solid underfoot, the blood
only a few blotted drops
where brambles had snagged on skin.
Come on, you said, *it's your move.*

II

'Two are brave and four are wise;
You yourself must be the seventh.'
— *Attila József (tr. John Bákti)*

The Protagonist

The story goes that there's a sword
up a gentle incline of hillside

and the power goes to whosoever
plucks it from the outcrop where it's planted,

but who's got that kind of time to spare
to test the tensile strength of a prophecy?

You say, *I'm so tired.* I say, *Snap.* I always say
when I grow up I want to be a main character,

at least a speaking part. Ha ha,
not likely, not in this economy,

but there's always a need for backdrop,
especially trees. I've taken to

wearing several black jumpers at once,
ideally cable knit. I want to fall in

with a crowd of philosophers. They'll tell me
the gaps keep heat from escaping. Let the space

itself be the protagonist. Let the table
be headless and ready for guests.

Washed Up by the River

The first baby had a note pinned to their swaddling. *Care for me* seemed clear enough. I left my galoshes to drip dry and bought a bulk of nappies. The second was less obvious: their basket was hidden among bushes near the supermarket carpark. That note had only a pictograph, a fish of some description, with horns. I wasn't sure the significance, but thought to go back to buy baby food, else I'd have to learn the methods of seabirds, my own grown-up meal recycled. The woman near the till directed me to a jar of orange paste—apparently bolognese and very popular. The third baby was incongruous on a middle shelf, as if customers were convinced in the baby aisle and halfway round thought, *actually, no.* They had a line of poetry tucked into their romper, which wasn't much use. What else could I do? I've had to take a second job as a night watchman at the sewage works. Minimal incidents mean there's been downtime to watch videos online and teach myself rudimentary metalwork, which I used to customise a pram, adding new rows. My parents have their own lives, and professional babysitters tend to hang up when they grasp the logistics, so I keep the babies alongside me everywhere I go, ensuring a slot's empty in case I stumble across another on the doorstep of a charity shop, or shelved among science fiction at the library. The seventh baby was the last with any instruction, a note made of shapes like writing, that writhed when I tried to read it, left me with a nascent migraine. Intermittently, the flat's filled with their glassy cries, though I'm certain I've kept them fed and clean and unconditionally loved. Without warning, one will look straight at me, as if they appreciate an important undertaking lies ahead of them, and they want to acknowledge my small part.

How I Keep Getting Myself

Weeks into a deadlocked city siege,
both sides waiting on my orders, exhausted
from sneaking in and out, swapping hats.
Now what? The battle for a slight edge
when it's obvious what I'll do next. We
excavated tunnels to undermine
their tunnels. All that granular dirt
crawled through just to begin from scratch.
Perfect counters for any attack,
saboteurs easy to spot; I recognise
each from their interviews.
Don't I know you? No
you do not. Trust me,
don't let in their huge wooden egg. It's an obvious trap.
Eggmen, retreat, they've seen through our trap.

A rousing speech twice over:
I promise we'll crack this, I promise we'll not crack.
An expert in attrition, famous for living
on tenacity alone for days, no-one questions
my regular disappearances,
assuming that to solo cry for hours
is part of the process. And it is—
when you're calling my name
and my gaze stays locked
on a nearby stack of rough sawn timber, like I am
zoomed right in, watching
tiny duplicates fight for their lives in miniature
between the grains, remember
it's a delicate game, to win without losing.

Posture and Grip

Shortly after my decapitation, I got this job
at Threadbare Removals Limited.
The duties are straightforward. I happen
to have a knack for squeezing through
narrow gaps. The head removal guy says
it's as if I lose my air like a lung
collapsed by an arrow, so I help
in loading the van. I can't drive
without incident, so I ride in the centre seat
as the skinniest, and team's most junior member.
At the other end, I do the same
in reverse. Beneath my black polo that's branded
with the company logo, I've taken to wearing a brace
for my back. Lifting with the legs. Each booking
fits neatly in a slot; bleeding over
costs double for the extra.
It's a job. When I'm off
for too long and it's quiet, I find myself
pacing the apartment, carrying a desk.
It belongs pushed back into the corner.
It's better under the window overlooking
the street. Or maybe in the centre
of the room like a hearth in a medieval mud hut.
I disregard the basics of manual handling
and tear through my stitches.

The Midwife

She's three quarters through, lugging swollen feet
towards the finish line. To qualify, a student
must deliver five hundred kids. That's enough

to rival Blackpool Tower, if measured as
a stack. Toast and strong tea in the break room
and back to the next lot of labours.

Till it takes on the nature of machinery:
an arcade pushing pennies.

Lucky parents find their footing instantly,
others look down as if standing on glass,
as if woken by a hypnotist to applause.

We're all sleeper agents awaiting activation.
The old is dying and the new cannot be born
without a beacon to head towards.

At home, her own baby is dreaming in his cot
but the hospital's third-floor ward endures
as a ribbon of light against the sky.

Spoils

At the end of the month, I turn in
my check sheet: a list of assorted heroics.
The clerk tuneless whistles and updates his spreadsheet.

A bushel of rare herbs acquired from a mountaintop.
A missing ring back in the hands of its owner.
A wagon escorted through countryside swarming
with bandits. The meeting notes logged, as requested.
I saved the townsfolk from themselves,
reshaping the truth on behalf of employers.

He tallies it all and deposits the funds in accordance
with work legislation and gains
made by unions. A portion's gone at once
for rent. And then the cost of eating.
I'd love to eat fresh, but I'm totally spent.

The driver is with me shortly. I take
my pizzas at the door. His fee plus tip
is the cost of him eating.
He'd love to eat fresh, but he's totally spent.

At home, he pours boiling water onto freeze-dried noodles,
to the pot's line, a little over. Green pea globes
and chunks of soya swirl, some make it
to the surface of the broth, some drown. Escaping
steam fogs his glasses and the kitchenette window.
Out there now could be something else entirely.

Apprentice/Master

It's a bit further, past this petrol station forecourt.
> *It scratched my forearm when I pulled free.*

What?
> *The chain link fence. I got my sleeve caught.*

You're bound to come by a scratch or two. I'm covered.
> *I can feel the air escaping.*

…
> *I'm deflating like a fairground prize hammer.*

Let me take a look at you.
> *The prize is fun until it bursts.*
> *But I never saw the point of the hook-a-duck. It's impossible to lose. You're paying to go through the motions.*

Your pupils always this size?
> *It's this new medication. Forever,*
> *two rippling black ponds.*

Look, it's literally a few more minutes and we're there.
> *A bizarre endorsement of pointless violence.*

What is? You said you were happy to help.
> *The ducks. They're stuck swimming in circles*
> *and then snatched from liquid safety,*
> *transactional. Only to be plonked back,*
> *skulls ringing.*

They're plastic. I don't think it's to be taken literally.
> *I guess it's more of a zero.*

A zero?
> *The circuit they're trapped in,*
> *it's not a circle. Sometimes*
> *it's a figure of eight.*

I think you're getting too entangled in this.
> *The symbol for zero holds*
> *nothing. The perfect*
> *expression of emptiness. What*
> *the hell is eight then?*

I left a casserole in the slow cooker. We should really be getting on…
> *How is a figure of eight*
> *symbolically appropriate?*

Don't sit down. You can sit down when we're done.
> *I'm supposed to just accept*
> *that's how things are?*

What if it's two sacks?
> *What if it's what?*

The eight is two sacks. One stacked on top of the other.
> *And in each sack is four?*

Exactly. It's obvious if you think about it.
> *Or two eggs together.*

Quadruplet ducklings in each one.
> *I hadn't thought of it like that.*

They're itching for the air.
> *We should get moving, right?*

Actually, that's not it, they want
to exist in continued ambiguity. It's like
their gift is in being undecided.
> *How do you figure?*

There is no winning. Or more,
we win by not playing.
> *I'm not following.*

Without the hook's interruption, everyone
bears the mark on their base, everyone
hides a grand prize.
> *A bit further right? Which way did you say it was?*

42

Oral History

Now everyone knows it, the king
was a fabrication all along, modelled
after dummies in department store windows,
gooey toffee compacted and sculpted,
with peaks and dimples by way of
facial features. No wonder

his appearances were rare and
always through gauze curtains. A kid
figured it out. We trekked into the capital
to corroborate—exactly as told:
his squishy majesty sat idling
not on a throne at all, but a mound
of bottles, cans and packaging
as if a party was

over. The castle we thought
must be theme park surplus
surrendered to our touch
like the skin of onions forgotten
at the back of the fridge. All those flags
only underwear, long since lifted by gusts
from the lines they'd been pegged on to dry,
discoloured by the seasons. The sudden

facts of it, inescapable. You might've heard
rumours, families flocking to the river mouth
to dispose of their silky clothes
and cover themselves in silt, the man
spotted marching with a bugle
to his lips, not blowing

but suckling, fixated; this new age
of enlightenment
has hit folks differently. But I've heard
tell of whole communities unaffected,

doormats where old news of regicide
is unwelcome. The king is dead, long
gone. The king never was. Whole
towns where the crier grips a silent bell

and bellows nothing: no week
of mourning. They awake
with the trees not draped in black
but leaves instead. I'm following

the smell of hot food through the woods.
These daily gummy supplements are no longer enough.

Hero Training

It might've ended with cuts, but
a consummate pro, he twisted the knife
free from the assailant's grip. Management
had his name engraved on a medal.
Before the ceremony, taught his eldest to tie a Windsor knot,
said, *You'll need this in future for interviews*

and funerals. At home,
he ignites the barbecue, hot enough
to melt the medal: silvery condiment
drizzled over hot dogs. *Tea's ready,*
everybody. Let the metal
coat your belly. When it cools,
you'll be harder on the inside.
It'll help with what they stick you with.

Hearth

When the blue-haired cat
visits from next-door-but-one,
the locket of me unclasps.

I can feel the steady boom
of his heart through fur,
till after a minute, he bats away
my hand, as if to say,

That's enough. The heat is too much.
His claws like an avuncular adult,
teaching a kid about the hob.
When I learned Granddad had died,

it was winter. The stark lines
of the trees were exposed.
At school, I held
a pair of red safety scissors
to my wrist
and said, *If he can't live,
neither should I.*

Now where does a ten-year-old learn
a trick like that? To open up
freely in front of a room.

A Path

For a while, I lived in the woods
on the outskirts. A space to lie
motionless and study the sky. But trees
are possessed of this singular viewpoint.
Their every conversation loops back
to sunlight, to water. I was flat
in the dirt and gulping through a bland meal
of lichen, when a series of thoughts occurred:
somewhere a bottle of ketchup is clinging
to the last splodges of itself; a couple
is sat round a sticky table, cursing
their respective managers; a dad and his son
are in the garden, setting off a rocket
they built with instructions from the internet.
I stood, then, shook off my coat of moss,
walked until I found a road and followed
a bus route back into the city, re-entering
from the west, passing below the railway.
When a train rolled overhead, the bridge
underneath sounded like the MRI machine
when we finally accepted it was time
to assess any damage.

III

'This is the Medicine of Life.
It helps you recover your Life.'
— *The Legend of Zelda: A Link to the Past*

The Agency

I ate the mushroom
growing on the wall of the downstairs toilet
in the house we rent. I folded
a thick slice of brown bread around it
and gobbled the lot raw. They might try
charging us extra at the end of our tenancy
because the mushroom wasn't meant for us.
But in their assessment, what is? See
what I have in my hands. It's nothing.

See it moving. Like devotees
bowing round a colourful altar.
They forbid us painting over the white
but I painted anyway on the white
of the sink with the rainbow
of my vomit. I am

thirteen again. I am hovering
a foot above the ground like a god. They don't want us
skating on their office block steps as if
the concrete isn't there for us. Smooth
as a dream of endless falling. Shouting
watchmen emerging to shoo us off the premises.
What are they thinking,
that they can contain this? It's only
my folded arms holding me together.
If I raise my hands towards the sky,
so bright and boundless I ache,
a thousand canaries will take flight.

Understudy

This again—my student has crammed
his pockets with gravel and
cannonballed into the reservoir.

Sopping, and cold as a milestone
on the bank, I take his word
this isn't about suicidal thoughts,

he saw the tell-tale green and gold
of treasure blinking on the bed
and isn't that what we're doing here?

Sure, but wouldn't growing gills
be covered during induction
if that was all it took? Tomorrow,

I'll pull him from a different waterbody.
We'll sit in the sun getting warmer.

Compulsions

In the waste ground over the back, that family
of hypnotherapists who moved in, how lovely
to swap our sightings round the breakfast bar—
I saw them pruning hedges, removing
chickweed, dock, you saw them unclick a footlocker,
their pocket watches, metronomes, all lunchtime
watched them placing uniforms on hangers,
semiformal but loose fits, calm earth tones, wire spectacles
down the bridge of their noses, constructing
their nests from green branches and saliva, the Fibonacci
spirals of the framework. In autumn gold, a bouquet
of sparkles bloomed on the chain link fence

and the room had gone dark without me clocking till you
said, *Don't you want this lamp on?* Yes, and I've quit smoking.

Aubade with Forecast

Winter morning spreads this blush over
the southeast, but it's overdue we outgrow
rosy cheeks and meekness. I have bitten
my chapped lips bloody once again, pink
ministers gesticulate with red palms
from the refuge of their motorcades and

despite it all, the sky is in attendance
daily. We have work to do. To be
or not? We want the scope to choose the former.
I need that answer as forearm tattoo for
when facing a limited palette. Today is okay,

up early to handfeed the guinea pigs radicchio
and kiss you as I leave. The horizon promises
spring and we'll get what's coming to us.

His Echocardiogram Looks Good Now

When daytime predators clock off and
larger night-time hunters aren't prepped yet,
they take the opportunity, the pipistrelles,
to wind a black helix through the evening.
I realise, while you're sat warm inside
—my shift again to let the dog piss—
what the trick is. You have to look sidelong
to recognise the flicker of their silhouette:
attune to the lamplight's yellow backing track
to notice the beat skip. And I smile,
scooping his mess into a poo bag, grateful
for restorative shocks. I know they're catching
insects too slight for me to see, yet I can't help
but think of them as revelling just to be
up there surrounded by the air.

Missing Years

If you're in the area, could you look out
for my missing bag, it's big and grey
and multi-coloured like everything is
from that era, but aside from that,
no distinguishing features, although
inside is a sword, you'll know it's likely my bag
if there's a sword in it, ornate and impractically large,
much bigger than has any right fitting in a bag that size,
but we all took on more than we were ready to,
a decade of bus tickets in origami stars or crumpled
into tiny paper planets, clean underwear too
and a bobbled towel in need of a wash and a toothbrush,
its bristles branching out like a system of roots,
no perishables left in pockets, I learnt that lesson
the messy way, hands in the mush of forgotten
bananas, and no, no baggies in the bag,
we stood, flushed, and let the plumbing slurp
each powder, tab, crystal, for the last time and
again for the last last time, my bag,
I had my oldest friend hold onto it, when
we were haunting that dilapidated factory,
the main hall, where fern fronds thrived in the brick,
chlorophyll slats interrupting the masonry,
defying conversion into swanky flats,
if you've gone far enough, you've gone too far.

Open Wide, a Little Wider

We were misled
by a sat nav quirk, the circle
sun at an unexpected inclination.
The country's vestigial tail,
you dubbed this snaking
A Road. Still inevitably
a wealth of luxury cars on hand
ready to elbow by, tinted window
undertakers, cutting us up and getting
a mouthful: *cunt, do your indicators not work
or are we invisible?* The final word flashing

in their rear-view. And then we turned a corner
and on the hill opposite was a line
of houses, a familiar-seeming close
in a town we'd never been. You said,
Who do you think lives there?
and I knew then someone
must, a street of someones, each
with their own purposeful face. I had
to chew on it in a lay-by: the abundance,
it won't all fit in my head. *But
that's the thing,* you said, *it doesn't have to.*

Something Came Up, Be There Soon

It's always a walk through the cemetery,
no matter where I happen to be working,
running late past weathered headstones.
You were right about geography deciding
the substance of connections with the dead.
That proximity never used to bother me
till the morning I met with the spectres
of what could've been but isn't,
the shape and size of butterflies, red smoke
just enough to fill the lungs of an infant.
I thought they were the colour of rust in water
till one rested on my thumb: curling vapour
like wings the shade of a low sun. I'm trying
to listen close and decipher their perfect speech.

Acknowledgements

The magic of *Human Townsperson* was made possible by a DYCP grant from Arts Council England.

Acknowledgements are due to the human townspersons at *Magma*, *bath magg* and *Spoonfeed Magazine* for publishing versions of some of these poems, as well as the human townsperson Velum Break, for creating audio for a video adaptation of 'Character Building'. More of his work can be found at https://velumbreak.bandcamp.com/

Endless thanks to Caroline Bird, human townsperson and cloaked mentor, whose patience, kindness and attentive guidance were invaluable for shaping this book and my craft more generally. A version of her editorial voice will live inside my head forever and for this I'm immensely grateful.

Thanks to the human townspersons I've worked alongside over the years: Paula and Barbara, long-time supporters and friends, who got me through some tough times unscathed and in Barbara's case were on hand for spontaneous Gramsci translations. And more recently, Chloe and Sara, who, having known me for not very long, were happy to spend actual money and time on books, merchandise and hearing me read poems.

Thanks to Roger Robinson, Andrew McMillan, Joelle Taylor and Luke Kennard, human townspersons who've given time, energy and words to reassuring me of my place on the poetry map.

Thanks to Bryony Littlefair, like-minded human townsperson who's been there with advice, recommendations, generosity and jokes.
Likewise, Miles Bradley, human townsperson and confidant, sensitive to my many complaints about the sparkly gems I've had to gather but have no idea what to do with.

Thanks to the human townspersons at Broken Sleep Books, Aaron and Charlie, and all the party members I'm honoured to now call friends.

Thanks to my family: Mom, Dad, Cameron and all of the extended whose love, care and support has helped make me the human townsperson I get to be.

Thanks to all the way back when human townspersons, loyal companions in misadventure, human side by side, whatever towns we quested through, whenever our personhood was in existential dispute. I love and miss you all.

Thanks to Katie, number one human townsperson, real life treasure and quest objective. I couldn't do any of it without you.

And thanks to Cosmo, who inspired the kind of love that people write poems about, in every human townsperson lucky enough to meet him. May his name go down in legend.

Hard as I've tried, doubtless there are human townspersons I should've thanked and haven't, so whether from a village or city or cabin in the woods, whether a tree or phantasm or cat, human townspersons all of you, thanks for joining me on this journey to the place it is we're going.

LAY OUT YOUR XP

Lightning Source UK Ltd.
Milton Keynes UK
UKHW012317270722
406465UK00005B/342